Jeshera
Whitehead

@Sheshegotfans
@supremu.yah

@ band0baby

@_famousDebo

Brandon
Jerrod
Jemadl
Sajaya

My Parents
Shermeka
Jemaall

grand Parents
Annette
george/Jb
James
Trisha

INVENTIONS

That COULD HAVE CHANGED

The *World* ... BUT DIDN'T!

Joe Rhatigan

• ILLUSTRATIONS BY ANTHONY OWSLEY •

imagine!
Publishing

10 9 8 7 6 5 4 3 2

An Imagine Book
Published by Charlesbridge
85 Main Street
Watertown, MA 02472
617-926-0329
www.charlesbridge.com

Text copyright © 2015 Joe Rhatigan
Illustrations copyright © 2015 Charlesbridge Publishing, Inc.
Interior and cover design: Melissa Gerber
Editing: Kate Hurley

Printed in China. Manufactured in July, 2015.

ISBN: 978-1-62354-024-1

For information about custom editions, special sales, premium and corporate purchases, please contact Charlesbridge Publishing, Inc. at specialsales@charlesbridge.com

CONTENTS

INTRODUCTION

If at First . . .

Take a look around you and try to count the number of inventions you see. Everything from the light you're using to read this book to the machines used to create this book was invented by someone who saw a problem and found a creative way to solve it. That's what inventions are: solutions to problems.

Some of these solutions have changed the world in fascinating ways. Before lightbulbs, people went to bed when it got dark outside. (There was nothing else to do.) Before the printing press, only a very few people had access to books. The very best inventions make you wonder how people ever lived without them.

There are a lot of great books about these incredible inventions and the fascinating people who made them. But this book has something else on its mind: What about the inventions that didn't change the world?

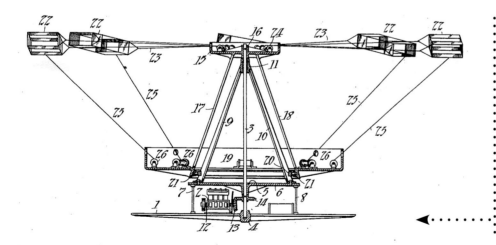

Thomas Edison, perhaps the most famous inventor ever, is known for his more than one thousand patented inventions. He isn't, however, known for creating this flying machine, which he patented in 1910. Why? It didn't fly.

4

The world is bursting with ideas. Unfortunately, not all of these ideas are good. For every amazing invention, there are thousands that are never produced, arrive too soon or too late to be of any use, or simply don't work. Some are too impractical, silly, or unwieldy. Others may be the next big thing . . . someday. In many ways, these flops can be just as fascinating as lightbulbs, cars, computers, and smartphones. Wacky, weird, wonderful, or just plain wrong, these are the inventions included in this book.

In some sense, you can say this book is about failure, but it's a kind of failure worth celebrating. The human race can't move forward without trying and sometimes not succeeding. Without these inventions that didn't work out, we probably wouldn't have the ones that did. So this book celebrates the flops and also-rans—the inventions that could have changed the world, should have made a difference, or would have astounded us all, but for one reason or another didn't.

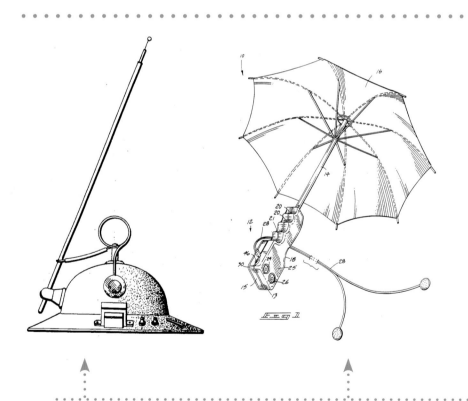

There were dozens of failed inventions before personal sound systems succeeded, including the Radio Hat, patented by Olin Mumford in 1948, and the Umbrella with Removable Radio Handle, patented by Joseph Divine in 1989.

In order to get credit for an invention you come up with, you need to get it approved by your country's patent and trademark office. In order to do that, you have to fill out a patent application and provide compelling reasons why your invention should be granted a patent. Many times, inventors include illustrations of their ideas. The black-and-white illustrations in this book come straight from the patent applications inventors sent to the patent office. The numbers and arrows in many of these illustrations refer to written descriptions in the patents.

For instance, the illustration below is for U.S. Patent #1494508, issued to Henry Smith in 1924 for a cane with wheels. In Figure 6 at the top, the number 7 refers to an opening to receive number 8, the bolt.

My collaborator, Anthony Owsley, is responsible for the color illustrations. He worked hard to make sure the inventions he drew looked like the real ones—although he also had some fun along the way.

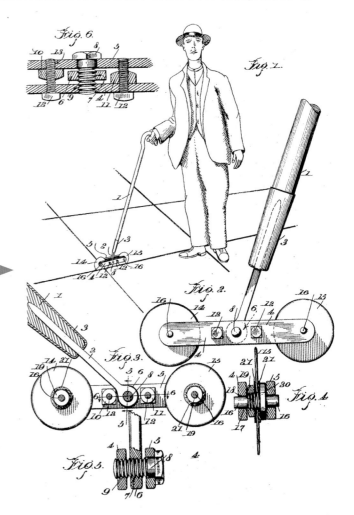

The World of Inventions and Patents

Nobody knows who invented the wheel, the compass, or even mirrors. That's because people at the time didn't think to record that information anywhere. (Or writing hadn't been invented yet.) Beginning in 1790, if you created a device or procedure that was different and useful and you wanted to make sure nobody stole your idea, you could apply for a patent. According to the United States Patent and Trademark Office, a patent is "an intellectual property right granted by the government . . . to an inventor to exclude others from making, using, offering for sale, or selling the invention . . . for a limited time in exchange for public disclosure of the invention when the patent is granted." Simply put: If you write out an application, pay the fee, and then the government grants you a patent, nobody can steal or make money off your idea for twenty years. Meanwhile, your invention becomes public and anyone can look at your application, learn from it, and perhaps create new inventions based on it.

FYI

The idea of patents has been around since the 1400s, and the first patent law in the United States was enacted in 1790. The United States Patent and Trademark Office grants more than 180,000 patents a year and so far has granted more than eight million patents. Meanwhile, the Canadian Patent Office examines more than 30,000 requests per year and has granted more than two million patents.

The United States Patent and Trademark Office is headquartered in Alexandria, Virginia, and employs nearly ten thousand people.

The first U.S. patent was issued to Samuel Hopkins on July 31, 1790, for an improvement "in the making Pot ash and Pearl ash by a new Apparatus and Process." The patent was signed by President George Washington.

Not all patents are approved. In fact, in order for your invention to receive a patent, it has to pass three tests.

Test #1: Is it novel?

In other words, is it new or does it have a new part that another inventor hasn't already thought of? You can't patent the paper clip because someone has already invented it. However, if you invent a paper clip that doubles as a nostril cleaner, you may be on your way to receiving a patent.

Test #2: Is it useful?

Does your invention have a practical use and can someone actually create it? In other words, you can invent all the time machines you want, but until you can shake hands with George Washington, you can't patent it.

Test #3: Is it inventive?

This means that your invention isn't obvious and couldn't have been thought of by just anyone with basic knowledge about the subject.

"The patent system added the fuel of interest to the fire of genius." —Abraham Lincoln lthough it's impossible to predict with certainty whether an invention will be the next great thing or a flop, these questions can help.

Does it work?

This one is obvious.

Does it do its job better and more cheaply than other inventions?

If something works better than your invention, nobody will want yours. Thomas Edison did not invent the lightbulb. He did, however, replace the oxygen in the bulb that others used in previous lightbulbs with gases that worked better. Also, he experimented with thousands of different filaments until he found the one that glowed the best and lasted the longest. Edison also invented the method of using the lightbulb in homes—making its use easy and affordable. That's why we remember his name and not those of his predecessors.

Do people want it?

A great invention at the wrong time can fail just as easily as a horrible invention. Chester Carlson invented the photocopier in 1937. During the next seven years, his invention was turned down by more than twenty corporations. In fact, it took more than ten years for him to sell his idea and another ten before companies were buying Xerox machines, making Carlson a millionaire.

Can you get the money to mass-produce and market your invention?

Many inventors have to rely on others to invest in (or pay for) producing their inventions in order to sell them. A great idea will just sit on a shelf without money to make it.

Are you lucky?

It can't hurt to be lucky!

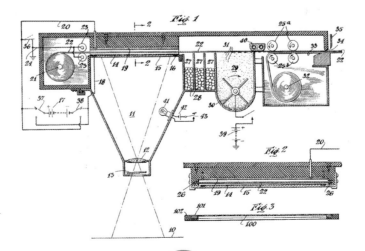

Carlson's invention was a flop . . . until it wasn't.

CHAPTER 1

Going Nowhere

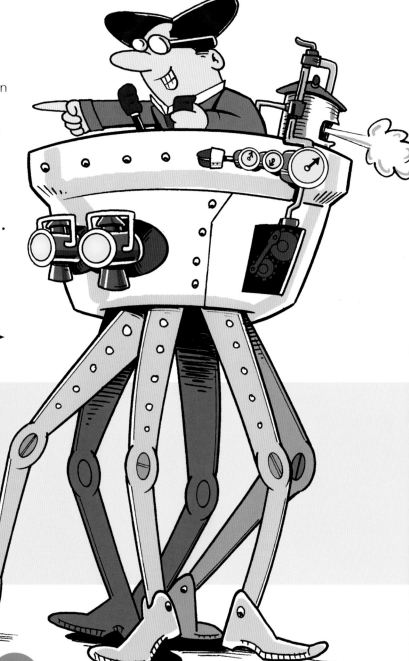

Humans have always been fascinated with getting places quickly, efficiently, and in style. And for every mode of transportation you can think of, there are countless inventions that never quite took off. Imagine what your trip to school might be like if one of the following inventions had succeeded.

◄ ·······································

The following inventions might get you where you want to go . . . but then again, perhaps they won't.

·······································►

"Just because something doesn't do what you planned it to do doesn't mean it's useless."
–Thomas Edison

The First American Horseless Carriage

As with many new inventions, the first person to do something isn't always the one who gets rich and famous. According to most historians, John W. Lambert invented and made the first gasoline automobile in America; however, not too many people know about him. The year was 1891, seventeen years before Henry Ford started producing his much more famous Model T car. Lambert's motorized tricycle had two speeds, no reverse gear, and three wooden wheels with steel rims. Although Lambert was never able to convince anyone to pay $585 for what he called the Buckeye Gasoline Buggy, Lambert and his horseless carriage were responsible for the first car accident. Lambert, out for a drive with a friend, hit a root sticking out of the ground. He lost control of the buggy and crashed into a post. Both driver and passenger had minor injuries.

Ford's First

In 1896, Henry Ford designed and built his first automobile, which was called the Quadricycle because it ran atop four bicycle wheels. It had two gears and could reach speeds of twenty miles per hour. It couldn't, however, go in reverse. Ford only built three Quadricycles and sold one of them. It would take another twelve years of experimenting before Ford would find success with his Model T, but his success with this early model led him to found the Henry Ford Company, which would eventually make him the richest man in the world.

The bicycle in your garage isn't much different looking from the first bicycles in the late 1800s, but that doesn't mean there haven't been some strange two-wheeled inventions.

Isn't It Dandy

The Dandy Horse or *Laufmaschine* ("running machine") was patented in 1818 in Mannheim, Germany, and is considered the first means of transportation using two wheels. In other words, it was the first bike. The Dandy Horse was very popular for a short time, until riders began hitting and hurting pedestrians. Within a year or so, the running machine and others like it were banned.

Fig. 1.

Row, Row, Row Your Bike

Patented by Louis Burbank in 1900, this combination bicycle/rowing machine looks like great exercise . . . As long as you don't have to steer. The object of the invention was, according to the patent application, "to provide means whereby one may enjoy with a bicycle or similar vehicle exercise like that of rowing with a pair of sculls, which is adapted to develop the muscles of the arms and body as well as those of the legs."

No Peaking

Theron Cherry, like most in the late 1800s, thought it improper for women to ride bicycles, lest their legs be viewed, causing scandal. This Screen for Ladies Bicycles, patented in 1896, protects a woman's feet and ankles from view when riding, and also keeps "the skirts from being blown about the limbs."

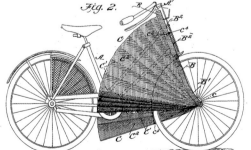

Fig. 2.

No Frame Needed

A patent was issued to Justin W. Trenary in 2004 for this "body-connected bike." The Body Bike was meant for downhill racing cyclists who don't want to bother with gears, pedals, a frame, or even a seat. So far, it has not been produced. According to the patent application, "the body of the rider acts as a connecting means between the front and rear roller assemblies and allows high-performance riding."

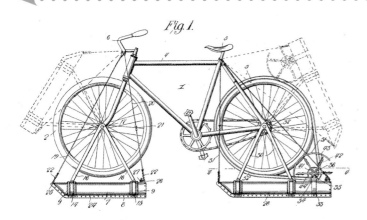

Pedaling the Pond

This 1912 invention by Henry Munsen could supposedly travel on both land and water. The dotted lines in the illustration show where the metallic floats would be while riding on land. Once on the water, when you pedal, the rear wheel turns a paddle wheel, propelling you forward. Cables connect to the handlebars and front floats help with the steering.

The Fliz

Before the modern bicycle was invented, similar contraptions were patented in which the rider had to walk or run while on top of the bike. These bicycles were called *velocipedes*, and they went out of favor once bicycles with pedals and chains became popular. Two German inventors, however, recently created the Fliz, a type of velocipede in which the rider is strapped to a frame between two wheels. You start it by running while holding on to the handlebars. Once you find yourself at the top of a hill, you can rest your feet on the back wheel. The Fliz was invented to encourage an alternative to driving.

Is One Wheel Better Than Four?

Early automobile inventors used carriages and coaches as inspiration for their designs, with some sort of compartment moving forward on top of four wheels. In the early 1930s, however, the British inventor Dr. John Purves decided to think outside the box by putting the car driver *inside* a single wheel. Purves invented a giant, ten-foot-tall, doughnut-shaped iron contraption that held a driver and three passengers. The Dynasphere, as Purves called his vehicle, reached speeds of up to twenty-five miles an hour during many demonstrations.

Unfortunately, those who watched this amazing wheel in action also noted the Dynasphere's driver had trouble steering, braking, and seeing the road in front of him. There was also a chance that the driver and his passengers would spin head over heels like a hamster that suddenly stops running in its wheel. These limitations kept the Dynasphere from ever appearing on our roads and highways.

Online
Watch the original Dynasphere in action: *bit.ly/1lo7NBK*

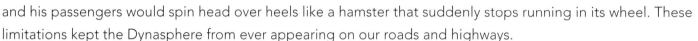

Leg and Arm Powered

Transporting yourself inside a wheel was a bad idea more than thirty years *before* the Dynasphere. With this contraption, patented by Thomas Tolson in 1897, you pedaled with your arms and legs and steered by leaning one way or the other.

14

How High Can You Pedal?

his flying machine, invented by Andrew Mraula, seems to have gotten its inspiration from the bicycle, as you pedal with your hands to turn the blades. Once the blades moved fast enough, you would be lifted into the air. Then you'd start pedaling for your life with your feet as well. Perhaps the best part of this scary contraption is you can fold it up when you're done and carry it on your back.

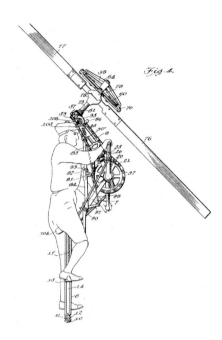

Need a Lift?

his nifty contraption, patented by Harold Bush in 1969, is part pogo stick and part helicopter. By holding the upright support in your hands and pushing down on the foot pedals with your feet, you can propel yourself in a series of high jumps and gentle, blade-driven falls back to earth. According to the patent application, "substantial flights can be achieved by descending a hill and tilting the blades so that the angle of attack is such that the device is airborne for a substantial portion of the hill. The pivotable wheel can be replaced by a ski member during the wintertime to provide a year-round amusement device."

The Jumping Balloon

The object of this invention, patented by Clarence Adams and others in 1925, was to produce a balloon "adapted to sustain the weight of a single passenger (who) with the aid of the balloon and propelling mechanism may perfect a jump from the ground to an altitude of several hundred feet. The balloon is particularly useful in jumping over buildings, trees, rivers, and chasms." The inventors imagined this device could be used to jump over buildings, trees, rivers, chasms, and more, as well as a neat way to take photographs and easily inspect rooftops.

The Car That Flew

Imagine sitting in traffic. Suddenly, with a push of a button, your car lifts into the air and zooms away. That's one of the reasons many inventors have spent their lives trying to come up with a car that flies . . . or a plane that drives. One of the more famous of these attempts was the Aerocar, built in 1949 by Moulton Taylor, an aeronautical engineer from Oregon who wanted to create the only plane you could drive to the store. The Aerocar was a two-person, boxy vehicle with foldable wings that could be towed behind the car when driving. In fewer than five minutes, the driver could convert the car to a plane and be up, up, and away! In driving mode, the Aerocar could reach speeds up to sixty miles per hour. As a plane, it flew up to 110 miles per hour. Taylor couldn't attract enough investors in his invention, and even though he marketed it for several years, none were ever sold. He only ended up building six Aerocars, some of which are now in museums.

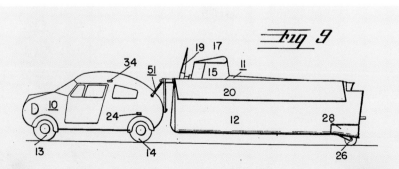

Henry Ford didn't invent the automobile, but his Model T and assembly line production method made the automobile cheap enough for people to actually buy. After this success, Ford wanted to create the Model T of the air. He called it the Flivver, and it was small enough to fit in the driveway and simple enough for anyone to fly. Prototypes were built in the mid-1920s, and the dream of highways in the sky seemed within reach.

During a test flight, the Flivver's engine stalled and crashed, killing the pilot and the whole project. It was later discovered that the crash was entirely avoidable, but Ford canceled the Flivver project anyway.

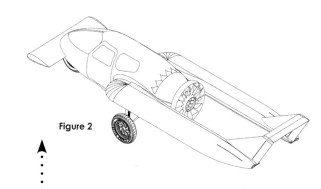

The Ford Flivver after a test flight

Will It Change the World?

Several inventors have tried to turn Ford's dream of an airplane in every driveway into a reality. Using the Flivver as inspiration, Lewis Blomeley patented this one-seater airplane/motorcycle in 2013. This "roadable aircraft" has collapsible wings, with no parts having to be removed and left behind when converting from motorcycle to plane. Do you think it will change the world?

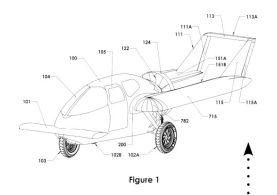

Figure 1

Figure 2

The Falling Tailor

The airplane was a new invention during Franz Reichelt's lifetime, and many pilots died when their planes broke down in the air. The Austrian-born French tailor and inventor decided to invent a parachute coat that would provide a safe way for pilots to exit a plane and fall to the ground safely. Reichelt's final prototype was a twenty-pound, cloak-like garment that was deployed simply by extending your arms. Reichelt tested several prototypes with dummies, but in 1912, when he thought he had it right, he decided to test out his parachute coat himself . . . by jumping off the first deck of the Eiffel Tower (187 feet). Even though friends tried to stop him, Reichelt said, "I want to try the experiment myself and without trickery, as I intend to prove the worth of my invention." He jumped, and unfortunately, his invention wasn't worth much: the parachute failed to open and Reichelt plummeted to his death.

Can Submarines Fly?

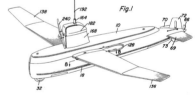

Imagine how incredible it would be to fly thousands of feet in the sky one instant, and then be underwater the next. Donald V. Reid, an engineer for an aircraft manufacturer, and his son, Bruce, decided to find out by building the first operational flying submarine they called the Reid Flying Submarine (the RFS-1, for short). Using leftover parts from crashed aircraft, Reid created several models before finally achieving flying and diving success in the early 1960s (patented in 1963). Unfortunately, the RFS-1 could only dive around twenty-five feet underwater, and it was so heavy that it could only fly for a few minutes at a time.

The Car That Swam

For nearly thirty years, German inventor Hanns Trippel created dozens of designs for a car that was also a boat. Finally, in the early 1960s, the Amphicar was designed and marketed in the United States, although only around four thousand were ever produced. The main problem was that it wasn't a very good car, nor was it a very good boat. Plus, there wasn't that much demand for a swimming car.

President Lyndon Johnson owned an Amphicar and liked to trick friends by pretending the brakes stopped working as he headed for a lake. The car would enter the lake, and instead of sinking, it would begin swimming.

Will It Change the World?

Bogdan Radu patented this flying, swimming, and driving vehicle in 2013. According to the patent, the vehicle stores its rotors (for flying) inside the body while the car is driving or in the water. When in the air, the rotors create the lift (sort of like a helicopter) to fly the vehicle. Radu invented the vehicle in order to "bypass congested roads, traverse water areas, and be able to fly over land or water." Do you think it will change the world?

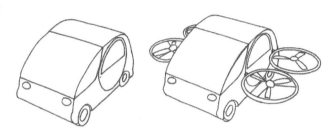

Toot, Toot! Time to Fill the Tank

Although not as famous as Thomas Edison, Lee De Forest had more than 180 patents, and was the inventor of the Audion tube, the first electrical device that could amplify an electrical signal. This helped make radio broadcasting, television, and long-distance telephone service possible. Known as the father of radio and the grandfather of television, De Forest is not, however, known for his Indicating Device for Fluid Tanks (patented in 1925), a gas tank gauge that blew a whistle whenever a car's gas tank got low. Although it worked, consumers decided that a gas gauge on the dashboard was a better invention.

Would You Like to Fly Like a Bird?

nventor W.F. Quinby was one of the many whose work with human flight led the way to hang gliders and eventually the first airplane, even though Quinby himself never got off the ground. Here are a few of his beautiful yet not-so-airworthy designs. (Due to Quinby's lack of understanding of how heavier-than-air flight was achieved, none of his inventions ever left the ground, and the inventor remained earthbound his entire life—even though it looks like he never gave up trying.)

The Flying Apparatus

Flying Apparatus, patented in 1867, presents Quinby's idea of attaching wings to the arms, along with what look like feathers attached to the rear. Quinby stated, "This invention relates to a new and improved flying attachment, whereby a person will be enabled to fly or propel himself through the air similar to birds. In using this invention, a motion is given the arms and legs almost precisely like that in swimming, and the effect is nearly the same."

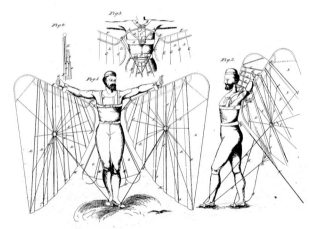

The Flying Machine

Quinby continued his quest to fly with the Flying Machine, patented in 1869. This invention was "intended to provide an arrangement of temporary sails resembling the wings of birds, which may be readily connected to the body of a person."

Improvement in Flying Apparatus

Quinby made further improvements to his flying designs in 1872. It doesn't look any safer! This improvement was to "support the flying apparatus entirely on the trunk of the operator and remove all weight from the arms and legs, so they will be free to give their entire strength to the operation."

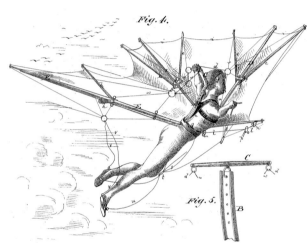

Aerial Ship

In 1879, Quinby added a wheel and some kites. His Aerial Ship also didn't leave the ground.

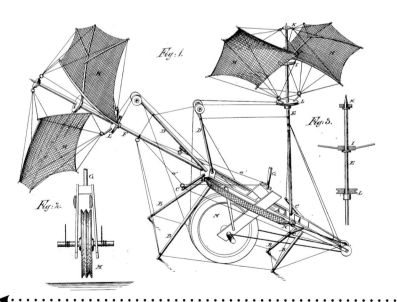

Driving the Future

An architect, inventor, and scientist who explored possibilities about the future, Buckminster Fuller invented a car (patented in 1937) that looked and acted unlike any automobile then or now.

Built in time for the 1933 World's Fair in Chicago, the Dymaxion Car featured two wheels up front and one in back. Shaped like a gigantic eggplant, it was twice as long as a normal car and could fit eleven people. The steering wheel controlled the back wheel, which made it extremely easy to fit into small parking spaces and perform U-turns. Unfortunately, one of the Dymaxion Car prototypes crashed during the World's Fair, killing the driver and injuring two passengers. This crash was enough to scare off any investors in the project.

FYI

The word *dymaxion* is a combination of the words *dynamic*, *maximum*, and *tension*.

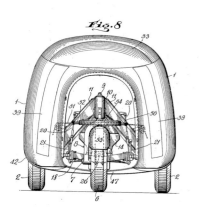

Fig. 8

Only three Dymaxion cars were ever produced, with the only existing model now at the National Automobile Museum in Reno, Nevada. This photo is of a replica built in 2010 by Norman Foster, who used to work with Fuller.

Why Not Go Nuclear?

Once the automobile was established as the best way to get from one place to another, carmakers kept making their vehicles better, faster, and more reliable. Years of research and thousands of hours of experimentation have gone into each part of the cars we drive today. However, not every new idea is worth pursuing. One such not-so-hot idea was the Ford Nucleon. In 1958, the Ford Motor Company wanted to create a car that could go five thousand miles without having to refuel. Wouldn't that be wonderful?

What wasn't wonderful was the small nuclear reactor in the car's trunk. The idea for the Nucleon was scrapped once scientists realized the potential danger of highways jam-packed with vehicles that could cause radiation poisoning and mushroom cloud explosions.

Rocket Packs for All!

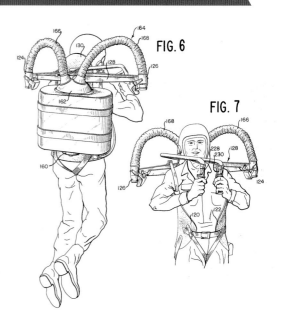

Science fiction writers came up with the idea of a rocket-propelled lifting device for people way back in the 1920s. However, as of 2014, we still don't have a reliable jet pack we can use to lift ourselves off to school or work. In the 1960s, the Bell Aerospace Corporation developed the Rocket Pack for the U.S. Army to use, and although it worked rather well, the Army canceled the project since the belt could only keep a person in the air for about twenty seconds. More than fifty years and several more attempts later, we're still waiting for our rocket belts. The rocket pack on the right was patented in 1966 by John Hulbert and Wendell Moore. This design weighed sixty-eight pounds and could fly 300 feet in a circle at about twenty feet off the ground.

Online

Go to this link to see the 1966 Rocket Pack in use: *http://bit.ly/1lJyB0M*

No Wheels Needed

For a while during the middle of the last century, inventors thought the next great way to get around would be without wheels, and magazine articles announced that pretty soon we'd all be driving on air instead of on the ground. The vehicle that promised a world of no more potholes was the hovercraft, most versions of which looked like small flying saucers with motorcycle handlebars.

American inventor Charles Rhoades created one such device called the Hover Scooter, which rode six inches off the ground and could handle any terrain, including roads, grass, dirt, and even water. So why were the magazines wrong? Unfortunately, hovercrafts are hard to steer, and if you drive too fast, you may lose the air under you and end up back on the ground. But the worst news for hovercrafters is that the only way to stop one is to turn off the engine and then wait until you slow down. So unless hovercrafts come equipped with anchors, there won't be much demand for them any time soon.

How Hovercrafts Work

Hovercrafts are simple devices that float on a cushion of air forced under the craft by a fan, providing the hovercraft the lift it needs to get off the ground. A skirt under the platform keeps the air beneath the craft. A motorized fan propels the vehicle forward, and rudders, such as the ones used to steer boats, are used for turning.

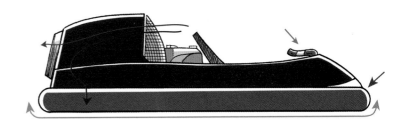

Make Your Own Hovercraft

What You Need

- A balloon
- A sports drink cap (that twists open and closed)
- Modeling clay or cyanoacrylate glue (such as Super Glue)
- A CD or DVD you don't need anymore

What You Do

1. Blow up the balloon and then attach it to the top of the closed drink cap.
2. Roll a piece of the clay into a thin snake and press it around the hole in the CD. (If you're using glue instead, skip to the next step.)
3. Press the drink cap onto the clay, making sure it's as airtight as possible. If you're using glue, place the drink cap over the hole in the CD and glue it into place, making sure to leave no space for air to escape.
4. Open the drink cap and give your craft a gentle push.
5. Next, try using different platforms, such as plastic plates, cardboard, or whatever else you find.

Online

Watch the Hover Scooter online: *bit.ly/1ktqlz4*

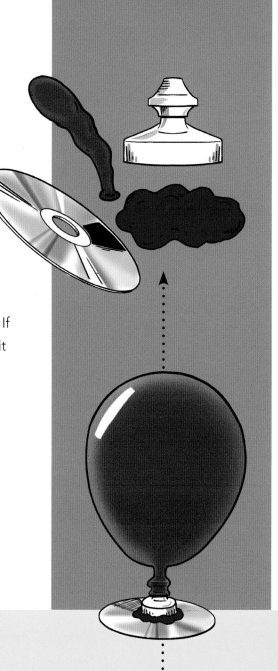

Here's an Idea!

How about a car with bicycle parts attached so you can pedal home if you run out of gas?

CHAPTER 2

Easier, Quicker, Safer . . . Weirder

People invent things for many different reasons. Early in his career, Thomas Edison decided only to invent things that would make money. Other inventors want to be part of creating a better world in which everyday functions such as brushing your teeth are done more easily and quicker. When an inventor succeeds, we get electric toothbrushes. When an inventor fails, we get the incredibly strange inventions in this chapter.

"I have missed more than nine thousand shots in my career. I have lost almost three hundred games. On twenty-six occasions I have been entrusted to take the game-winning shot, and I missed. I have failed over and over and over again in my life. And that is why I succeed."
—Michael Jordan

U.S. PAT. ELECTRIC EAR WAX REMOVER

Imagine what life would be like if these inventions did change the world.

Concrete Dream Home

It would take a whole book to list all of Thomas Edison's accomplishments. Inventor, businessman, and hardworking genius, Edison developed the long-lasting lightbulb, and invented the phonograph (which recorded and played back sound) and the motion picture camera. He also made several innovations in electricity, concrete, and more. With more than a thousand patents to his name, Edison helped create the motion picture industry, the recorded music industry, the electronics industry, and more.

However, not every idea of Edison's was a smash hit. One of his failures included cement homes, complete with cement furniture and even pianos. In the early twentieth century, Edison wanted to provide cheap houses for low-income families, and he thought that creating homes from a single mold into which cement was poured would be a great idea. He dreamed of a future where millions of Americans lived in these practically indestructible, fireproof, and bug-proof homes that could be poured in a single day and ready to move into several days later. Nearly a dozen homes were built using this technique in 1917 in Union Township, New Jersey, where they are still lived in.

Unfortunately, the mold was too expensive for builders to afford. It included up to 2,300 different parts that needed to be put together before it could be used to pour the homes. Maybe if Edison's mold had been much simpler, you and all your friends would be living in concrete homes.

Thomas Edison showing off a model of his concrete house design

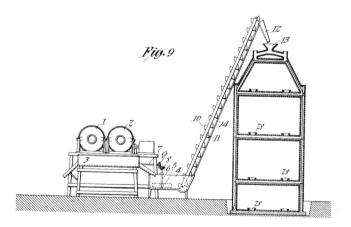

Is It Possible to Talk to Ghosts?

Known as the Wizard of Menlo Park (where his New Jersey laboratory was located), Thomas Edison would have had to be a real wizard to create an invention that would talk to the dead. But according to a magazine article from 1920, that's exactly what Edison was trying to do. In the article, Edison said, "I have been at work for some time building an apparatus to see if it is possible for personalities which have left this earth to communicate with us." There is no evidence the device was ever built or that, if it was built, it worked.

How Powerful Is Your Voice?

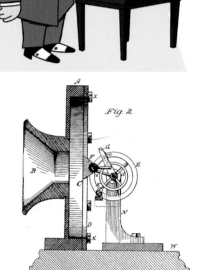

Patented in 1878, the Vocal Engine, or phonomotor, was one of Edison's weird failures. The Vocal Engine attempted to use the energy of voices to power a small engine. For instance, say your electric wall clock had stopped. All you would have to do to get it going again would be to speak into the mouthpiece (labeled B in the diagram to the right). Your voice vibrations would turn the wheel (labeled E), which, when connected to a belt, would drive a machine.

But one voice, no matter how much it is used, does not have enough energy to set anything in motion. According to author William M. Hartmann in his book *Signals, Sound, and Sensation*, it would take "one million people, all talking at once" to light a sixty-watt lightbulb.

Eat 'n' Wash

Dishwashers have become a near necessity in today's kitchens. Since it was first invented in 1850, there have been many, many patents that improved dishwashers to the point where they are today. However, not every patent has been helpful. This 2000 patent by Harold DeHart combines the dining room table with the dishwasher so you would no longer have to "transport the dishes to and from the table." Simply eat and place the dirty dishes in the washer underneath the table.

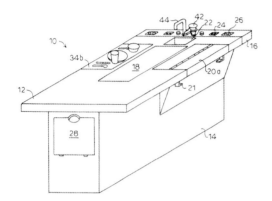

FYI

The first reliable dishwasher was invented in 1886 by Josephine Cochrane. She didn't have to wash dishes herself, but she invented her device to prevent her servants from chipping her dinnerware.

Ejection Notice

Having trouble getting up in the morning? Do you simply ignore your alarm clock? Of course you do! That's why this bed was invented by George Seaman way back in 1892. The bed is wound sort of like a clock, and is attached to an alarm clock. Once the alarm goes off, the mechanism under the bed is triggered, and the bed's occupant is "spilled upon the floor." You will only oversleep once.

All Snug on a Bouncing Rug

The next time you're staying over at a friend's house and have to sleep on the floor, remember that in 1976, Donald Stephens knew your pain. He devised a rug with an inflatable backing that, when inflated, became a rug-covered mattress. Imagine the fun if we all had one of these!

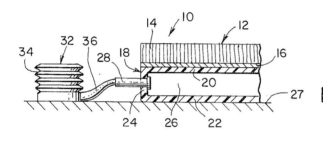

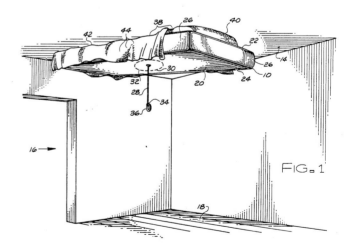

Fig. 3

Bed in the Clouds

Your bedroom only has so much space. Wouldn't it be great if you could store your bed somewhere until you needed it at night? How about the ceiling? This patented, but never produced, invention is basically a floating bed. Inventor William Calderwood imagined filling the mattress with helium so your bed would rise when you do. When you need it, simply reach up for the tether, pull it down, and hop on it before it floats back up. The inventor imagined that just about any piece of furniture could rest on the ceiling until needed.

FIG. 1

Ride and Watch

Have you ever felt guilty for just sitting around watching TV instead of doing something like exercising? Have your parents ever told you to get off the couch and go outside and ride your bike? This invention, called 123GoTV, takes care of all that by making you ride a bike to power the TV. It's an exercise-activated switch that includes a bicycle mounted on a stand. When you pedal the bicycle, it sends a signal to the switch, which turns on the TV. Patented in 2011 by Margie Mullen, the 123GoTV was produced, and as of 2012, around fifty had been sold. For some reason, the 123GoTV is no longer for sale.

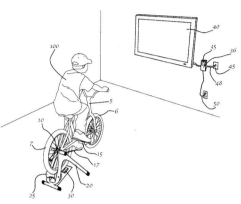

Online
Watch an original TV commercial for 123GoTV here: *bit.ly/V23tAp*

Dog Run

You can burn a lot of calories jogging or walking, but your arms are just sort of hanging there while your legs do all the work. How rude! Inventor Richard Reinert decided to fix this "problem" with his 2001 invention, which is a treadmill for your legs *and* arms, "similar to four-footed animals." A belt around your waist holds you up as you bend over and gallop your way to fabulous fitness.

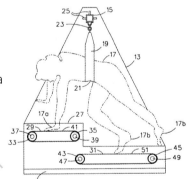

FYI ◀ ◀ ◀ ◀

People started inventing exercise machines in the late 1800s, and one of the most successful inventors was Gustav Zander. He built dozens of machines, including this velocipede motion apparatus, to help people develop all the muscles of the body. Many of his basic designs are still in use today.

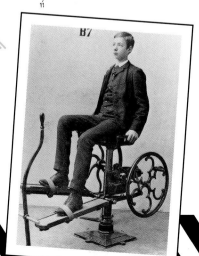

Living in Bucky's World

Buckminster Fuller developed and improved several inventions, including the geodesic dome structure. Although originally invented after World War I by Walther Bauersfeld, the geodesic dome was perfected and patented by Fuller in the 1940s. The dome is constructed using a pattern of connected triangles to form a structure that encloses the greatest amount of space with the least amount of surface area and is quite strong. Fuller's domes have been used for auditoriums, weather observatories, storage facilities, museums, hotels, and sports stadiums.

The Biosphere is a geodesic, dome-shaped museum dedicated to the environment in Montreal, Canada.

However, Fuller's Dymaxion Houses never caught on. Like Edison before him (see page 27), Fuller wished to create a home that just about anyone could purchase. He designed a few different prototypes, all of which (with the proper project funding) could be ordered by mail and delivered to where you wanted to place it. The design included a round, aluminum-covered structure with a waterless toilet, a fogger instead of a shower, revolving dresser drawers and storage shelves, a water-recycling system, and more. One reason his homes never changed the world was that they looked so weird—as if they belonged in a science fiction movie, not in a neighborhood.

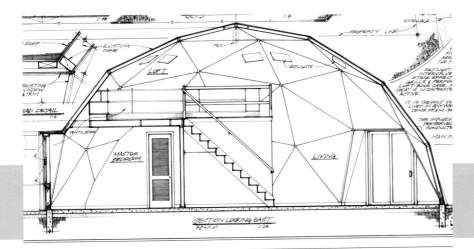

Assembled in approximately seven hours on Tuesday, April 19, 1960, this was the plan for Buckminster and his wife's private residence, called the Dome Home. It was the only one ever built.

Online

Go to the following link for more information on Bucky Fuller: *bit.ly/1nudWw0*

Make Your Own Dome

What You Need

11 gumdrops or other soft candy

Toothpicks

Paper plate

What You Do

1. Build a pentagon with 5 of the gumdrops and 5 of the toothpicks.
2. Using the gumdrops and toothpicks, build a triangle above each toothpick in the pentagon.
3. Connect the gumdrops of these new triangles with toothpicks.
4. Stick one toothpick in each of the gumdrops at the top of your structure. Lean them toward the center and then join them with a gumdrop. This is a simple dome. If you want to make a bigger structure, make your base larger and build around it.

FYI

Bucky Fuller felt that the death of his young daughter in 1922 was due, in part, to the damp and drafty home they lived in. He then had a vision in which he was floating above the ground bathed in a sphere of light. A voice told him that he belonged to the universe and that, if he applied himself, he could change the world. So began Fuller's journey to write, create, and invent.

Would you want to live here? This is an early prototype of Fuller's Dymaxion House.

Food Flops

As we move faster, doing more and more, with barely any time to make our own meals, food companies and inventors have tried to come to the rescue with food that's easier, quicker, and, hopefully, delicious (although that doesn't always seem to matter). Here are a few tasty treats that didn't quite make it.

Toasted

Toasters are mainly used for toasting bread. But that hasn't kept companies from trying to come up with other things that can be toasted. After the success of Pop-Tarts in the 1960s, inventors came up with Toaster Eggs, Toaster Chicken Patties, and Toaster French Fries—none of which succeeded. The best attempt, however, has to go to Reddi-Wip's Reddi-Bacon, which was precooked bacon in a foil pouch that you simply dropped in the toaster. Unfortunately, fat sometimes leaked from the pouch, causing a fire hazard.

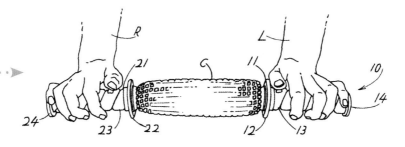

Corn on the Hog

Tired of Junior not eating his veggies? How about attaching motorcycle handles to a corncob? This invention, if ever produced, would do much, much more. The handles, when activated, rotate the corn and make motorcycle noises. Although this patent was granted to Nicholas Kretschmer way back in 2001, this awesome invention has yet to be produced.

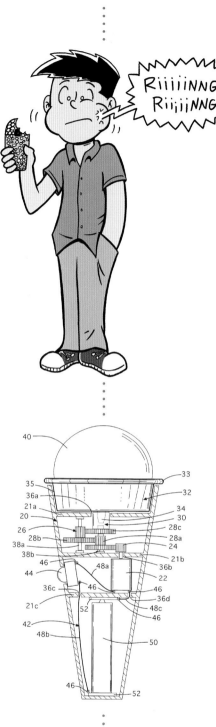

Just in Case

For $81, you can now purchase an edible smartphone case. Made entirely of rice cake, the Senbei Rice Cracker Cover is made in Japan and is "great in an emergency when you are desperate for a snack." Unfortunately, the case will probably break if dropped, but you have five seconds to pick it up and eat it.

Adult Baby Food

In 1974, Gerber released Gerber Singles, which were larger servings of their baby foods. These weren't for larger babies, though—they were aimed at college students, who were smart enough to veer away from this product.

Ice Cream Drone

Is rotating your ice cream cone as you eat it too much effort? Well, with this invention, patented in 1999 by Richard Hartman, all you have to do is stick out your tongue and let the device do all the hard work for you as it turns the ice cream 'round and 'round.

Food with Feet

This 1969 invention is for anyone who never understood why hot dogs are "dogs." It's a hot dog with dog legs. Unfortunately, inventor Edward Kiwala failed to invent the bun to go with these dogs.

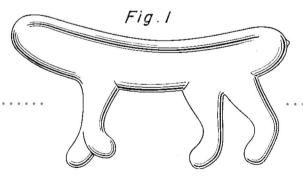

Fig. 1

Do Babies Need a Window View?

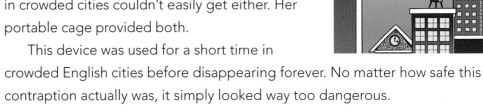

Living in a cramped apartment in a busy city? Do you feel like your baby needs more sunlight than she is getting? Try the Portable Baby Cage! Patented in the United States by Emma Reed in 1923, the Portable Baby Cage is exactly what it sounds like. Simply suspend the cage outside your window, make sure all the supports are in place, and drop the baby in. The baby is then free to take in the sights from the eighteenth floor. The inventor thought correctly that babies needed plenty of sunshine and fresh air to develop properly, but realized children born in crowded cities couldn't easily get either. Her portable cage provided both.

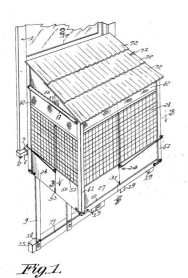

Fig. 1.

This device was used for a short time in crowded English cities before disappearing forever. No matter how safe this contraption actually was, it simply looked way too dangerous.

Do Dogs Need Toy Dog Vacuums?

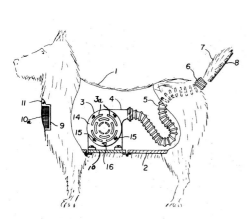

Most dogs don't like to take baths. Many also don't like getting their hair cut. They'll jump, whine, and sometimes even bite. This 1973 invention by A. Zaleski was meant to calm these poor creatures while they're being groomed. What is it? On the outside it's a realistic-looking toy dog. However, inside is a vacuum meant to suck up a real dog's recently cut hair from its body. Once a dog's hair has been cut, the groomer would turn on the vacuum dog and pull out its tail, which acts as the vacuum's suction hose. Since the vacuum is disguised as a dog, the real dog shouldn't freak out … unless seeing another dog's tail pulled from its body while making sucking sounds is something that would bother your dog. By the way, the tail end can be converted to a blow dryer as well.

Putting the Kids to Work

With this invention, kids could start earning their keep before they're even out of diapers. This pedal-operated lawnmower, patented by Deanna Porath in 1984, combines exercise and mowing lawns into one fun activity. Although, if you're young enough to still be riding a tricycle, you're also probably young enough to get seriously hurt by this contraption.

Is It a "Crush" or a "Bromb"?

Tolbert Lanston invented this combination comb and brush in 1871. This was designed "in such a manner that both operate on the hair at the same time." Unfortunately for the inventor, this combination just wasn't seen as needed.

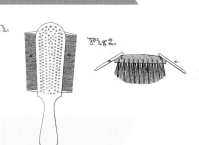

Baird's Bizarre Inventions

John Logie Baird was a Scottish scientist, engineer, and the inventor of the first television that transmitted a moving image. While considered one of the 100 Greatest Britons, this honor was not bestowed on him for his earlier, not-so-successful inventions. These unsuccessful inventions included: a glass razor, which although rust-resistant was not shatter-resistant; inflatable shoes; and the Baird undersock, which was basically a sock you put on before you put on your socks for extra warmth.

FYI ◄ ◄ ◄ ◄

Tolbert Lanston became much better known as the inventor of a mechanical typesetting system to replace the difficult task of hand-setting every letter when printing a book.

Inventing a useful means of escaping a dangerous fire inside a building is a noble cause. However, it's probably not such a great idea to invent something that could cause more harm than the fire.

Safety Hat

Benjamin Oppenheimer's Improvement in Fire Escapes was patented in 1879, and the description of this contraption is best left to the inventor himself: "This invention relates to an improved fire escape or safety device, by which a person may safely jump out of the window of a burning building from any height, without injury and without the least damage, on the ground. It consists of a parachute attached, in suitable manner, to the upper part of the body, in combination with overshoes having elastic bottom pads of suitable thickness to take up the concussion with the ground."

Safety Wings

In 1909, Pasquale Nigro, an Englishman living in Tennessee, thought wings would provide a better means of escaping a burning building. He stated that once the wearer strapped on the wings, "the air imprisoned beneath the fabric material [serves] to uphold the wearer and break the force of his fall."

Will It Change the World?

This Fire Escape Parachute was patented in 1998 by Yu-Li Yu and has yet to be produced. Do you think it will change the world?

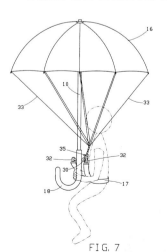

FIG. 7

Rappel to Safety

This 1893 invention by Orville Matts was meant to be a portable device you bring with you when visiting a tall building. If the building catches on fire, you hook the device to a window ledge, snap the body belt around your body, place a foot in the stirrup, grasp the friction roller gripping device, and sail downward rapidly and safely—much as a cliff climber rappels down a slope.

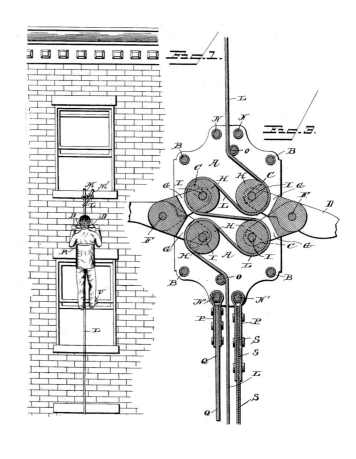

FYI

Although fire escape chutes can be found on some old buildings, using a slide-type enclosure to quickly escape a building never really became all that popular. They certainly look like fun, though!

Here's an Idea!

How about a building with fire escapes that double as a full playground for kids who don't live close to a park? If a fire ever breaks out in the building, the kids will know exactly how to escape.

Lollipops for the Lazy

Even though the idea of putting food (especially sweets) on a stick has been around since the Middle Ages, the Bradley Smith Company of New Haven, Connecticut, was able to patent the term LollyPop in 1931, after producing the hard candy on a stick since 1908. Since then, inventors have been coming up with delivery devices for the delivery device—things that hold the stick that's holding the candy.

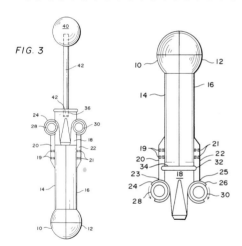

FIG. 3

Pocket Pop

This device, patented by Thomas Coleman and three others in 1996, acts as a lollipop "stick" that also folds up over an unfinished pop, protecting it from dirt.

Froggy-Pop

Peggy Levay patented this lollipop device in 1997. Put this contraption in your mouth and it looks like you're eating a frog, mouse, or other creepy critter.

Fowl-lipop

The inventors of the Pocket Pop above also came up with this dandy in 2000. Why? Because everyone wants a "limp feeling" chicken lollipop.

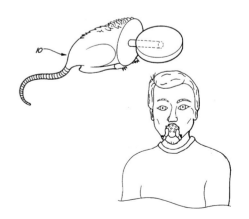

Cell-ipop

Jules Schecter received a patent for this device in 1997. This contraption records and plays back messages. It rings. It also stores a lollipop antenna, which you can pull out of the phone when you need a treat.

Pop and Pop

A patent was granted in 2003 to Al Cecere for this combination lollipop/drinking straw/beverage bottle cap. You have to suck on the lollipop candy for a while before you can get to the drink. Then, you get to enjoy the drink and the pop at the same time.

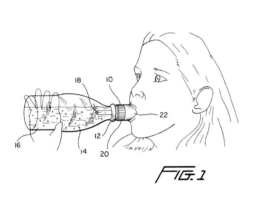

FIG. 1

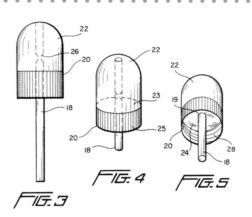

FIG. 3

FIG. 4

FIG. 5

Jewel Pop

If you can't finish your lollipop in one sitting, you can use this device, patented in 1995 by Sandra J. Wyzykowski, to store … and wear … your candy until next time.

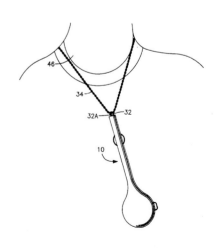

Twin Spins

The Thomas Edisons of the lollipop world, Thomas Coleman and gang (see above), were granted a patent in 1997 for this device for when one lollipop just isn't enough. When turned on, the contraption spins the lollipops for you.

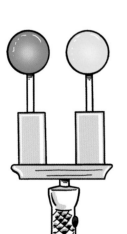

Lady Edison Goes to the Beach

Beulah Louise Henry wasn't married to Thomas Edison, but she was called Lady Edison from the 1920s through the 1970s because of the number of useful items she invented. Over the course of her life, she patented more than forty inventions and had at least seventy more she never patented. Some of her inventions include a duplicating device for typewriters (it made up to four copies as you were typing) and baby dolls that could be bathed and whose eyes changed color, as well as innovations for sewing machines, can openers, and office machines.

Henry with Miss Illusion, a doll with eyes that could change color and close

As with the other great minds in this chapter, not all of Henry's inventions caught on. One such item was the Parasol Bag. The next time you're at the beach, think of how difficult it is to carry all your stuff as you plod along in the sand. You need your shoes, towel, book, beach blanket, sunscreen, chair, and umbrella. Henry came up with an umbrella that also doubled as a bag to carry all your stuff. Patented in 1926, the Parasol Bag failed to catch on, even though most beachgoers wouldn't mind having one.

Two Ears Are Better Than One

Tired of passing the phone back and forth with his wife while talking to their son, Roger Heap invented and patented this contraption in 1952. The t-shaped plastic device fits over the earpiece of the (now old-fashioned) phone receiver, making three-way conversations simple and fun.

Weird Beard

There are several inventions for making sure your sideburns, mustache, and beard are neat and even; however, this one, patented by Scott Bonge in 2011, takes all the guesswork out of crafting your goatee (a beard that only covers your chin). Adjust the shaving guide to the desired shape, place it in your mouth, clamp down on the mouthpiece, and shave away.

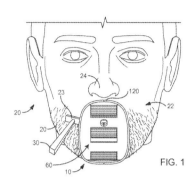

FIG. 1

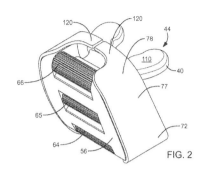

FIG. 2

How Will Your Hair Fare?

This 1992 invention, patented by Kim Jin, is for people who take great pains in selecting the proper hairstyle. Instead of imagining how a new look will look, simply stick your face in one of the cardboard hairstyles, check yourself out in the mirror, and decide if this is the new you. This invention would work for hairstyles or for people wishing for a wig or hairpiece.

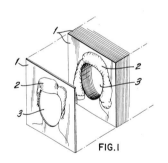

FIG.1

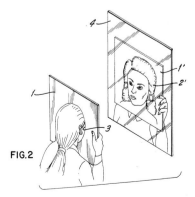

FIG.2

Here's an Idea!
How about a combination toothbrush, hairbrush, and ear cleaner?

CHAPTER 3

Fun & Games

We love to be entertained, and inventors are always looking for ways to show us a good time. They invent games, toys, sports, as well as new ways to experience movies and music. Only a very few of these ever make it to market, and of those, only a very few ever get noticed. The very best make the inventors millionaires. The rest end up in a book like this that celebrates how much fun these could have been … would have been … but sadly, aren't available for one reason or another.

"All I did was come up with what I thought was a fun idea [and] it just grew and grew and grew." —Ralph H. Baer, inventor of video games

Have fun, but be warned: the toys, games, and overall fun in this chapter have not been tested. You may set yourself on fire at band practice, get smacked upside the head with a ball, or play with a doll so creepy it will disturb your dreams.

Can You Take Your Hamster with You?

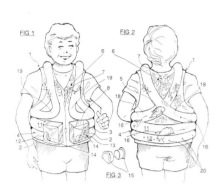

Dogs get to go on walks. Cats prowl around the yard or through the house. But what about hamsters, mice, and other little critters? They're stuck in cages! Inventor Brice Belisle tried to free these little guys to go where their owners go with this pet vest (patented in 1999) that's fun for you and your pet. With pet containers instead of pockets, and interlinking tubes that travel across the wearer's torso, the roving rodents could burrow, chase each other, eat, and look at the sights while you walk around town or sit in social studies class. Sadly, this invention was never produced.

Make Yourself at Home

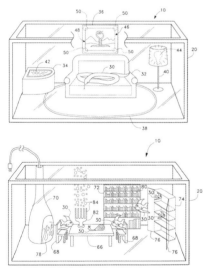

Feeling badly for your pet snake, fish, or other small pets for having to live among rocks, shells, and other annoying natural items? Well, give them the "human-like living quarters" of this 2001 invention by Olivia Terry and Lauren Dipolito. Your pet snake can lounge on a mini couch or sit by the fire. Or, your fish can enjoy a candlelight dinner before deciding what to read from the bookcase. Who said animals can't be sophisticated!?

Here's an Idea!

How about an aquarium jacket? It will keep you warm and distracted . . . although it's also going to be quite heavy. And stay away from knives and other sharp objects. And don't fall down. And beware of cats and seagulls.

You have probably come across all sorts of toys, stuffed animals, and dolls that talk or otherwise make some sort of noise. Well, Thomas Edison was ahead of his time with his Talking Doll, which ended up a dismal failure back in 1890 (patented in 1888). Edison, working with other inventors, shrank his phonograph invention until it could fit into a toy doll. Kids whose parents could afford the $10 ($25 with a fancy dress) to purchase the doll (about one month's salary for most Americans back then) would turn a crank in the doll's back to hear a nursery rhyme.

There were so many things wrong with this poor doll that it's difficult to know where to start. First off, since the recording industry was still in its infancy, the recorded nursery rhymes were difficult to hear and many of them screeched and scared the children. Children also had to turn the crank at just the right speed, otherwise the rhyme would come out either sounding like the Chipmunks (too fast) or Charlie Brown's teacher (too slow). Also, the wax recordings wore out quickly, the dolls often arrived in stores already broken, and perhaps worst of all, the dolls' tin bodies were not cuddly at all. Edison later remarked that, "the voices of the little monsters were exceedingly unpleasant to hear." Of the 2,500 dolls produced, only five hundred were sold.

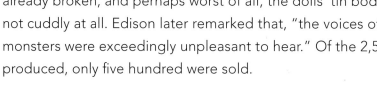

Online

Hear what one of the dolls sounded like here: *1.usa.gov/1hFEJVD*

Happy Face, Sad Face, Scary Face

Thomas Hong invented this re-configurable doll in 2008, and it comes with a blank face and plenty of lips, eyes, ears, and noses, which you can place on the face. Like a more cuddly Mr. Potato Head, this doll also has more expressions than the taters, although it's hard to tell what the doll in this illustration is feeling.

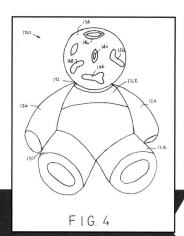

FIG. 4

Banana Face

There isn't much information on the patent application for this 1992 doll designed by Otto Alber. It's just a doll with a banana for a nose and shrubbery for hair.

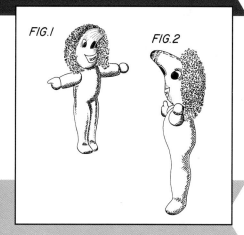

Run the Other Way

When you see this doll coming your way, run! Patented in 1915 by Louis Aronson, it emits sounds and moves, much as Frankenstein's monster did. Simply press on its stomach, and prepare to be scared . . . very scared.

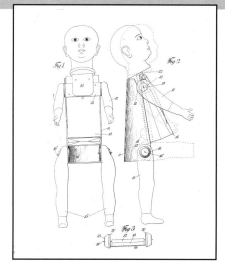

ny one of the following games could have become the next national pastime, as popular as base-ball, tennis, or football. Unfortunately, for one reason or another, they didn't.

Headaches Galore

In 1967, this patent was granted to Arthur Ryan, who took the saying "Just use your head" in a very different direction. The Head-Mounted Rebounding Device was invented to provide "enjoyable and beneficial physical activity . . . in which you project a ball . . . through the air without use of the hands."

Aim Carefully

Patented in 1989 by Wilfredo Diaz, this game/device is just like soccer or hockey, except the goal isn't on a poll or behind the goalie—it's between the goalie's legs. What could possibly go wrong with this setup!?

Soccer Knights

Here's another goal-protecting game, but this one uses shields to keep the ball from the goal. No lances required. R. Danford Lehman and Michael Williams patented this game in 1985.

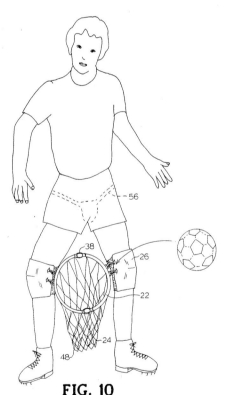

FIG. 10

Waist-Ball Anyone?

W. Walker was granted a patent for this game in 1973. This is a game of skill in which "the first player manipulates his waist to swing the ball upwardly to the level of the second player's waist, and the second player manipulates his body to catch the ball in one of the openings of his device." It also seems like a good game for young people to "mix and communicate with each other."

Wrist-Ball

How about a game of what looks like wrist volleyball?

Patented in 1960 by Georgia Glintz, this device was created to develop "the coordination of muscles" and "skills in the judgment of distances."

Hip Hip Game

Ralph Flanders patented this game in 1981. We have no idea what's going on with this contraption, so here's what the patent application says: "An exercise and game apparatus in which a ball having shafts attached thereto is rotatably mounted by the shafts within a hoop. Two attachment bars extend diametrically outwardly from the hoop and are secured to devices on belts around two people using the apparatus. Handles on the bars are provided to assist in steadying the apparatus as a revolving movement of the person's hips causes the ball to spin within the annular ring. Baskets may be provided on the attachment bars so that the people using the device can throw a ball back and forth, attempting to throw the ball into the basket on the opposite side of the hoop while continuing the hip movement necessary to keep the ball spinning."

No Bounce, No Dunk

This creation, patented by John Blue in 1997, is one part basketball, one part badminton, and one part crazy fun. Called Air Ball by the inventor, the ball must be hit to your opponent's side without bouncing, and the object of the game is to get the ball into one of your opponent's nets.

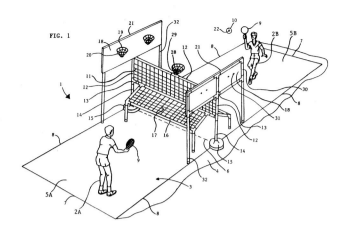

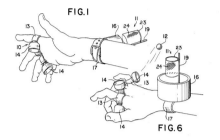

Hand Hoops

Who needs a court or a basketball hoop or even feet when you can play this basketball game with just one hand? Aida Sweeney and Patsy Boccardi patented this hand-version of basketball in 1964.

Basket-Foot Ball

Harvey King, perhaps tired of having a plain-old basketball hoop in his driveway, patented this contraption in 2002. This novel backboard allows you to shoot a ball like a basketball or pass it through the top net like a football for more points.

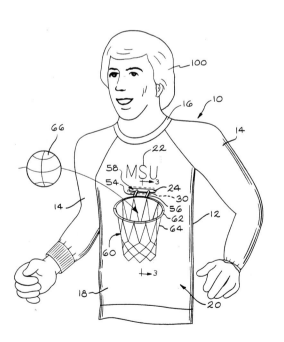

A Sure-to-Get-Hurt Shirt

Kirk Bristor invented this shirt in 1993 so you could bring the game of basketball with you wherever you went. Just don't let anyone dunk on you.

Two Noses Up

Imagine a car screeching to a halt in a cloud of burnt rubber and exhaust. Or a bad guy smoking a big cigar. When moviegoers walked into the Cinestage Theatre in Chicago to see the 1960 movie The Scent of Mystery, they were promised a movie that would not only show cars and cigars, but also let you smell them.

That's right: This mystery had action, suspense, and scents. The process of adding aroma to a movie was patented in 1956 and was at first called Scentovision and later changed to Smell-O-Vision. The invention included perfumes that were mechanically released during certain scenes in the movie. Fans would then blow the aromas into the theater. Unfortunately, most of the reviews of Smell-O-Vision were rotten. The contraption made a weird hissing noise, moviegoers in the back didn't smell the aromas until after the scene was over, and the odors didn't go away, they just mixed with the other odors, so soon the theater smelled like everything and nothing at the same time.

FYI

Another smelly invention called AromaRama released aromas into a movie theater's air-conditioning system. It, too, failed to catch on. One magazine called the competing inventions the "Battle of the Smellies."

Will It Change the World?

Dr. Kenichi Okada of Keio University in Tokyo is working on a desktop printer that will deliver odors instead of ink. Okada believes his invention could reinvent the way we view movies, TV shows, advertisements, and even old photographs. Do you think it will change the world?

Power to the Pogo

Speaking of pogo sticks, how about one that has a fully operational engine that runs on gasoline? This invention, patented by Gordon Spitzmesser in 1960, was called the Hop Rod, and the engine did the bouncing for you. All you had to do was stand on it and get bounced around. Even though advertisements said the Hop Rod was "extremely safe and harmless and tons of tremendous entertainment value," safety concerns kept it from being the biggest thing since the Hula-Hoop.

Online
Check out the commercial for the Hop Rod here: *bit.ly/1hbyWbJ*

Ski for Three

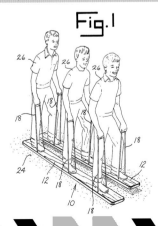

Fig. 1

Charles Marsh patented this shuffling-type toy in 1976 to help kids develop teamwork and coordination. Races could have been fun, too.

Cube-ism

Everybody wants to have fun, and there's no better way than inventing a game, toy, or idea that is so much fun that everybody wants to buy it. Imagine, for instance, being the inventor of Rubik's Cube, the three-dimensional puzzle game. Erno Rubik patented the device in 1983, and more than 350 million cubes have been bought. It was an instant sensation, and it continues to be popular more than thirty years later. Now, imagine being Larry Nichols, who patented a similar cube-like device in 1972. His toy looked like a Rubik's Cube, even though it was smaller, and you played with it in much the same way. However, it didn't catch on, even though it also looks like a lot of fun. He even tried suing Rubik and his toy company for patent infringement, but lost.

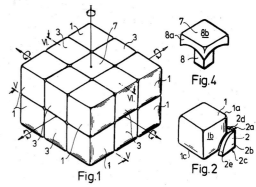

Nichols' Cube (left) vs.
Rubik's Cube (above)

FYI ◀ ◀ ◀

It took inventor Erno Rubik one month to solve his own invention.

Is Your Playing Hot?

Burn down the house with this trumpet (patented in 1981 by Pat Vidas) that not only helps you play the hottest tunes, but also emits, upon request, a large, controlled flame. Whatever you do, make sure you're not a second-chair player!

Food Should Be Fun

T he inventors of the following foods think food should be exciting and fun. What do you think?

What Color Is Your Ketchup?

Around 2000, Heinz, the condiment company, introduced EZ Squirt, a collection of colored ketchups, which included Blastin' Green, Funky Purple, Stellar Blue, and Mystery Color (which could be orange, teal, or purple). The ketchup came in squeezable containers so it was easy to "draw" wacky shapes and faces on your food. At first, these weirdly colored ketchups did okay, but eventually, families tired of purple fries and green burgers, and EZ Squirt was discontinued.

Will It Change the World?

With his 2005 patent application, Daniel Witkowski wanted to make eating fun once again by turning your soup or cereal into a game of skill. With this invention, you can link noodle monkeys together, put together a noodle puzzle, write a noodle sentence, create a noodle face, and more. Since "food is something to inspire imagination and provide entertainment," why not also make it interactive!? Do you think it will change the world?

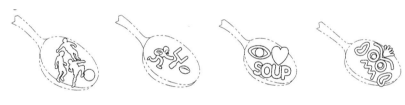

Which is your favorite?

FYI ◄ ◄ ◄

Alphabet-shape pasta noodles have been a hit with kids and adults since the 1880s, when they were first introduced.

Carbonated Milk

There's milk, there's soda, and for a short time in 2009, there was Vio, the world's first (and perhaps last) carbonated milk product. The makers of Vio called it "100-percent different," as well as "the world's first vibrancy drink." It contained 15 percent of your daily calcium and came in these fruity flavors: Citrus Burst, Very Berry, Peach Mango, and Tropical Colada. Unfortunately, it was full of sugar and didn't taste all that great.

Really Hot Dog

The only thing better than a hotdog is a hotdog with the feet, tail, and head of a dog! Edward Coleman patented this novel idea in 1960. According to the patent application, "the parts may be readily detached from the edible frankfurter and the frankfurter may be eaten if desired."

Eat Your Toys

Playing dolls can make a person very hungry. Valerie Gardner decided to help out these poor, hungry kids with this 1998 invention: clothing and other accessories for dolls that can be eaten.

Hot Dog Pretzel on a Stick

Patented in 1990 by Robert M. Kempher, the hot dog pretzel on a stick was certainly meant for state fairs and carnivals. And although you can buy pretzel dogs in some grocery stores, you'll have to add your own stick.

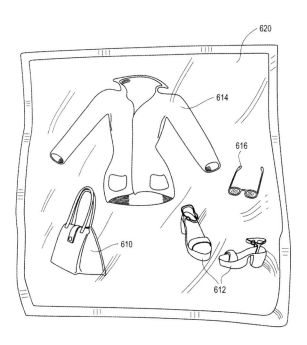

Built for Two

Nobody would ever be cold or wet again if all our coats could expand into Double Coats. Patented in 1953 by Howard Ross, this coat was meant for people caught in a storm at outdoor sporting events. If Double Coats were around today, we'd wear them everywhere … wouldn't we? Imagine playing tag, jumping rope, and going through revolving doors in one of these!

Forget the Suntan Lotion!

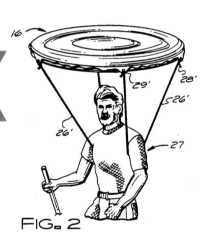

FIG. 2

Patented in 1991 by Frederick Sevilla, this helium-filled sun shade will protect you from harmful ultraviolet rays. Simply attach the giant, flat, disc-shaped balloon to your clothing or your beach chair, and bring the shade with you wherever you go. Don't forget your helium tank!

Who Needs Binoculars?

Although most people are perfectly okay watching birds and other flying critters from a distance, this 1999 invention by David Leslie guarantees you a front-row seat. Simply put this bird feeder contraption on your head—and whatever you do, don't sneeze!

Fun in the Tub

After a fun-filled day, wouldn't it be awesome to take a nice bath? Around the late 1800s, rocking baths were all the rage. The thinking was that if you couldn't get to the beach and enjoy the ocean waves, you could create some of your own waves in the comfort of your home. Sitting in water wasn't just considered relaxing back then, however; it was also supposed to be good for your health. Known as hydropathy, this belief that water can cure ailments was quite popular for at least fifty years, with water cure centers opening in Europe and in the United States. To cash in on this craze, Richard Straube invented the bath on the left in 1899 so people could get the benefits of these water centers at home. This model, when emptied, could also be used as a rocking chair.

Unfortunately for rocking bathers, no matter what the advertisements said, water got everywhere. Otto Hensel came to the rescue in 1900 with the rocking bathtub on the right, which featured a neck curtain that kept the water where it belonged.

Even though rocking baths fell out of fashion fairly quickly, hydropathy, which is now called hydrotherapy, is still popular with physical therapists, who use water jets, whirlpool baths, hot tubs, mineral baths, and more to help their patients recover from injuries.

An advertisement from September, 1891, extols the benefits of rocking in your bath.

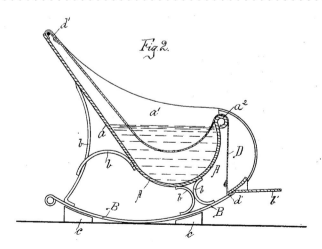

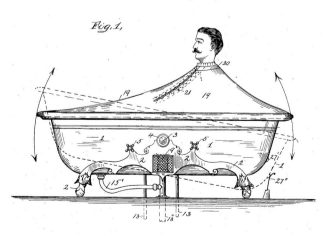

CHAPTER 4

Bringing up Baby . . . & Fido

The first thing you'll probably notice about the inventions in this chapter is that they don't make babies' and pets' lives any better—in fact, in some cases, they're dangerous. These inventions are for the people who have to take care of the babies and the pets: the parents. From toilet training and picking up pet poop to learning to walk and making sure you don't run away, the inventors of the following devices think they know how to enrich the lives of children, animals, and parents everywhere. What's interesting, however, is how similar many of the inventions for the babies are to the inventions for the pets.

You and your animal friends will thank your parents for not using any of these contraptions!

"One of the things that really surprised us is that adult dogs behave toward their caregivers like human children do." –Dr. Lisa Horn, who studied how dogs treat their owners similar to the way young children treat their parents

Take a Stand

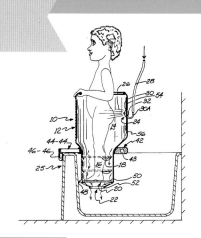

For most babies, bath time is fun time, with splashing, playing with toys, and getting your hair washed. But for parents who don't want to get wet, it can be a hassle. Jack Paden attempted to come to the rescue with this 1991 invention. It's a container you place in the bathtub that acts as a mini-shower for the child. Plop the kid in, hose him off, and you're done.

Baby in a Bucket

Here's a similar invention, with a much more frightening illustration, patented in 2000 by Frances Tuoriniemi and two others. The invention is simply a long bucket a baby can practice standing in while immersed up to the waist in water. According to the patent application, "baby feels herself lighter in water and is encouraged to stand. If the baby loses balance the walls will support her from falling." The premise of the invention is that a parent can take the baby in a bucket into the shower with them.

Got Soap?

Tired of chasing your dog or cat, holding him down, and spraying him with soap and water, all while getting bitten and scratched? Perhaps it's time for a Pet Shower. Patented in 1997 by Brian Moore, this device is a compartment that's hooked up to your home's water line. Simply put your pet inside the device, close the door (making sure your pet's head is sticking out), add soap, turn on the water, and sit back while Fido gets a shower he won't soon forget!

Who Needs a Helping Hand?

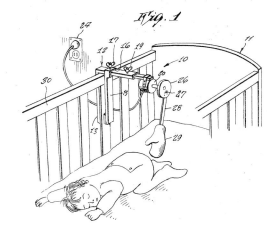

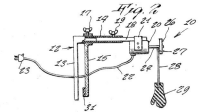

Thomas V. Zelenka of Hanford, California, patented the Baby Patting Machine in 1971. According to patent documents, Zelenka wished to create something for those poor parents who "must resort to patting the baby to sleep by repeated pats upon the hind parts thereof." Instead of spending all that time patting their baby's bottom, parents need only install the mechanical arm with a soft pad at the end to do the patting for them. Good night, kid, and hello Netflix! This invention was never produced, most likely because too many things could go wrong leaving a baby alone with a machine like this, thus saving a generation of kids from weird dreams of getting spanked in their sleep.

Will It Change the World?

For parents who need an extra set of hands, they can now keep them free with a Zaky Infant Pillow. Invented by Yamile Jackson, these pillows are the shape, size, and weight of human hands, and if you put them in the clothes dryer for a few minutes, they'll even be warm. They're flexible and can go over, under, and around the baby, helping him feel comforted and supported while his parents nap in the next room. Yamile's 2008 patent application is still pending. Do you think it will change the world?

Canine Petter

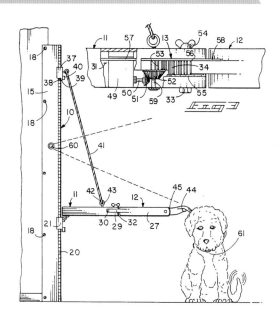

What does your doggy do when you're not home? Who gives him attention? Doesn't he get lonely? To keep your pet from realizing he's alone when you're not around, Rita Della Vecchia invented this device in 1989, which gives your dog some loving when you're at school and your parents are at work. The application states that this invention "provides a mechanical device to simulate petting for pets without requiring human attention." When your pet walks onto the base, the petting and scratching machine turns on.

Feline Scratcher

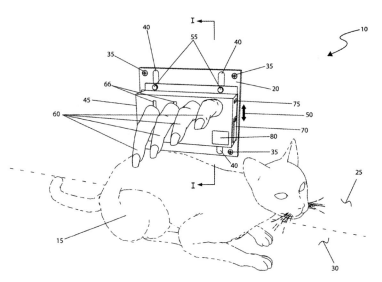

This scratcher, patented by Allison Schmuck in 2012 provides cats with four motion-activated fingers covered with a latex material so that they feel like real fingers. The device would be mounted on the wall, and when the cat came up to it, the fingers would start moving, giving the cat "entertainment, companionship, and solace when the owner is not present or available."

Too Pooped to Walk Your Dog?

The worst part about walking your dog is when you have to pick up his business. Sure, you could just leave it there, but that's usually against the law, and it's gross. Some of the following inventions that attempt to make picking up dog poop less work should also be against the law!

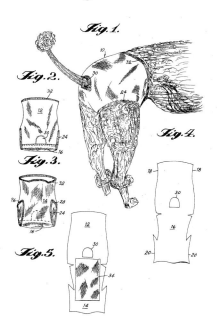

Diaper Dandy

This doggy diaper, patented in 1965 by David Hersh, was intended to "prevent damage to household furnishings occasioned by their exposure to animal wastes and to conserve time and energy in housebreaking a dog."

Keeping Them On

Dogs don't like diapers and tend to tear them off. This invention, patented in 2010 by Dorice Krenkel, includes two straps that help keep a dog's diaper in place.

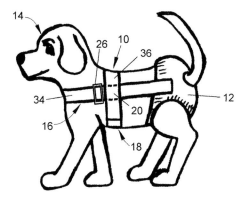

Swish

This 2013 invention by Melvin Powell is like a game of basketball. It provides a net with a disposable bag that can be placed right where the dog is about to go. Aim correctly, and swish! Two points!

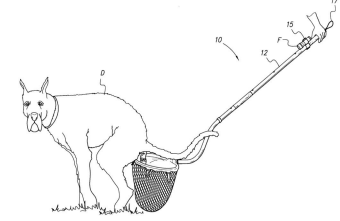

FIG. 1

Going Just Like Us

This idea patented in 2004 by Chui-Wen Chiu was never created, and perhaps you can see why by looking at the illustration. This was proposed as a flat platform with side walls to protect the room the toilet is placed in. When flushed, water would rush over the platform, removing whatever was there. The patent didn't specify who would do the flushing, the dog or its owner.

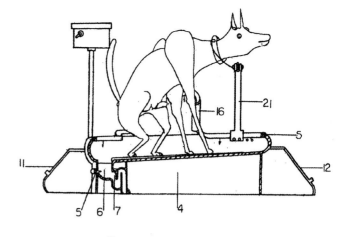

FIG 3

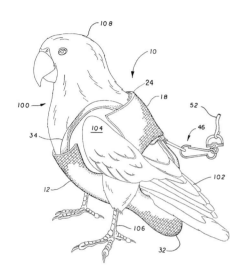

FIG. 1

Polly Wants a Diaper

Patented in 1999 by Cely Giron and two others, this is a bird diaper for an un-caged pet bird. A removable leash is also included so the bird doesn't fly away for good once you put the diaper on him.

Where Cats Plant Their Business

Tired of regular cat litter boxes that house-guests could stare and grimace at, Ronald Evans patented this device in 1993. It's a litter box disguised as a plant and flowerpot. The cat enters through a hole in the "pot" and does what he has to do while you enjoy the fake plant on top.

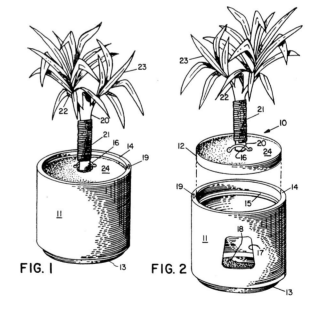

FIG. 1   FIG. 2

The Scoop on Kids and Poop

Much like pets, little kids are great to have around except for the whining and the pooping. Whereas we have to take care of animal poop all the time, children learn to do it themselves at some point. There are many inventions around to help this process.

Encouraging Words

Learning to go to the bathroom by oneself is an important achievement in a little kid's life, and parents are usually very impatient to get the whole process over with so they don't have to change diapers anymore. Unfortunately for parents, neither of these inventions took off. The Automatic Talking Potty, invented by Glory Hoskins in 1996, senses when a child is sitting on the potty and then talks to him. One sample message could be, "Big boy (or girl), you have used the potty. Now it is time to go wash your hands. Very good."

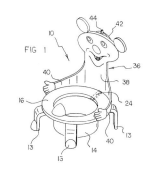

Toilets in Disguise

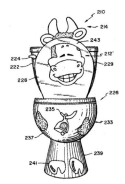

FIG.5

This invention by Joseph Lalicata, patented in 2007, is brilliant in its simplicity. Parents need only place decorative stickers of a cartoon figure on the lid, bowl, and bottom surface of a regular toilet bowl. The fun stickers will comfort kids when it's time to go (unless a goofy cow isn't comforting to you).

Will It Change the World?

A company in Brooklyn, New York, thinks little kids will stick to potty training if they're properly amused. They created the iPotty, which is a plastic potty with a stand for an iPad. Although the iPotty has only been on sale since 2013, it has drawn a lot of attention, including from child experts who say that an iPad provides way too much stimulation for kids who should be paying attention to what they should be doing and where they should be doing it. Thankfully for anyone else in the family who wants to use the iPad, the iPotty comes with a removable touch screen cover to "protect the tablet against messy hands and smudges." Do you think it will change the world?

Got It Covered

Have you ever seen how miserable dogs are when they have to walk in the rain? Have you ever smelled a wet dog? Yuck. Irinia Zhadan-Milligan and Yuri Zhadan came up with this dog umbrella and leash, which they patented in 2005. When it stops raining, the closed umbrella folds onto the leash.

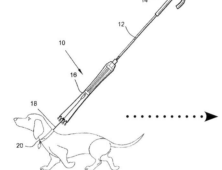

Fig.1

Got It Way Covered

Meanwhile, this 1992 invention by Celess Antoine lets dogs do their business on rainy days while their owners stay inside. Simply attach the device to the dog's midsection, positioning the covering so the dog can breathe, and watch your pet frolic in the rain, dry as a bone.

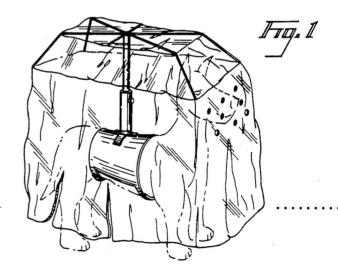

Fig. 1

Put Your Baby to Work

In Japan, there is a fad called *chindogu*, which is the art of creating totally useless—and usually fake—inventions. *Chindogu* inventions include the butter stick (a glue-stick-like device filled with butter that you rub on bread), and the all-day tissue dispenser (a toilet roll attached to the top of a hat). One famous *chindogu* was a baby's Onesie outfit that also doubled as a floor mop, which let crawling babies help out with housework. Some people, finding the fake advertisement online, wanted one so badly that the kind folks at www.betterthanpants.com obliged, making it for real. So far, sales have been strong, but until someone proves that dust-covered babies are a good thing, this fad will fade quickly.

Online
The Baby Mop in the news: *abcn.ws/1fFemia*

FYI

Chindogu means "unusual or weird tool" in Japanese.

Here's an Idea!
How about attaching a small vacuum to the baby so when he crawls on the carpet he can clean that, too?

Dog Walks Man

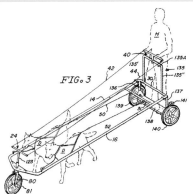

FIG. 3

This 2005 invention by Philip Kortuem is a dog-powered, human-controlled vehicle. The dog walks its owner, but the owner does the steering. It's great for Arctic exploring and racing, or for long walks around the park.

Fetch! Sit! Carry!

Why should you have to carry everything around with you when your perfectly capable dog can share the load? Sylvan Caditz patented this pet backpack in 1997.

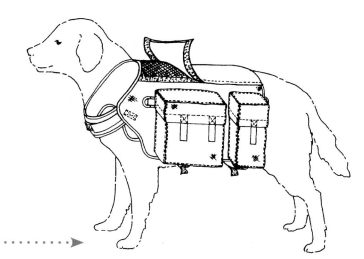

Fig. 1.

Can Cats Flush?

Indoor cats pretty much take care of themselves. Feed them and clean up their poop, and they're set. This invention, patented in 1972 by Michael Mcgee, teaches cats to use human toilets, eliminating the need for a litter box. The cat's potty training begins by first placing an oval-shaped litter box over the toilet bowl. When the cat gets used to this new arrangement, the first litter box is replaced with a box that has a hole in the bottom, so the cat's business falls into the toilet.

FIG.4

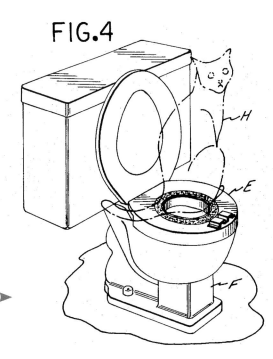

The Wubby Wire

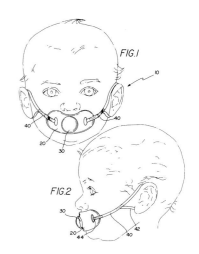

FIG.1

FIG.2

The illustration alone is enough to scare any parent away from this device, which is supposed to keep a pacifier in a baby's mouth (whether he wants it there or not). The Pacifier Securing System, which was patented in 2000 by Constance Chamberlain, includes a pacifier with adjustable straps that attach to the baby's ears, keeping the pacifier in his mouth and off the floor.

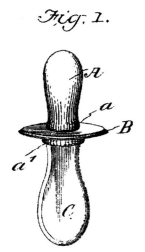

Fig. 1.

FYI

Although homemade pacifiers have been used for centuries, the first patent for what could pass for today's design was issued in 1900 to Christian W. Meinecke from Jersey City, New Jersey. Meinecke patented at least three designs for pacifiers, one of which was meant to be a superior design to a pacifier patented by Thomas Borcher, also of Jersey City, New Jersey. Strange!

Ears a Funny One

Animal ear protectors, patented in 1980 by James Williams, protect the ears of long-haired dogs from falling into their food while they eat. The dog's ears are pushed through two tubes, which keep the ears clean and out of the way.

Will It Change the World?

With dog obesity becoming more of a problem, inventors are looking for ways owners can help their pets get more exercise without the owners having to exercise with them. One such invention is a toy gun that shoots doggy treats (or lion treats). This design, patented in 2013 by J. Clarke Anderson and two others, hasn't been produced yet; however, there are a few similar designs on the market. Do you think it will change the world?

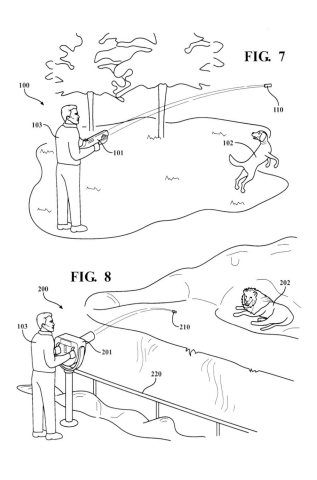

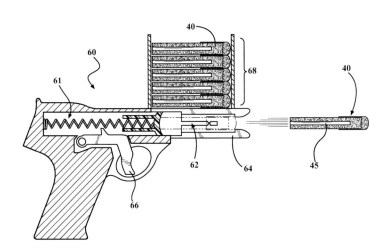

Here Comes the Scary Face!

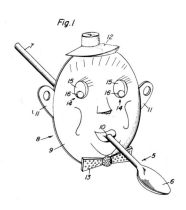

Parents will often play games with their babies to get them to eat their dinner. For children who are on to their parents' game of "open up, here comes the choo choo train," inventor John Wertz came up with this spoon in 1957. The face hides the parent's hand completely, making it look like a clown with a spoon in its mouth is heading straight for your mouth. Nothing scary about that, is there!?

Inventors often come up with their ideas when they see someone else's invention and realize they can improve it. Even though most babies figure out the whole walking thing on their own, inventors have been trying to help them out for at least a hundred years. Check out how an idea in 1920 led to an invention in 2011.

Fig. 1.

"A simple, cheaply constructed but thoroughly efficient device for assisting babies in walking." Patented in 1929 by Fred Stoll.

"An exercising device for an infant, which will enable it to practice walking without danger of overexertion or injury to its back or limbs." Patented in 1920 by John Bowden.

A device invented in the 1930s in Switzerland that, thankfully, never caught on.

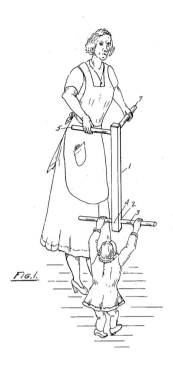

"A baby walking and balancing device."
Patented in 1951 by Joseph Spiteri.

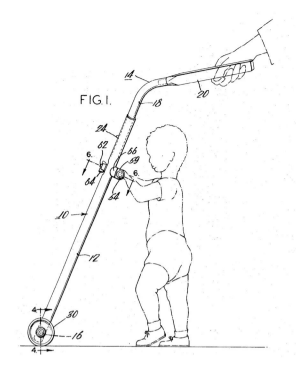

"Training device for aiding infants to walk."
Patented in 1970 by John Blank.

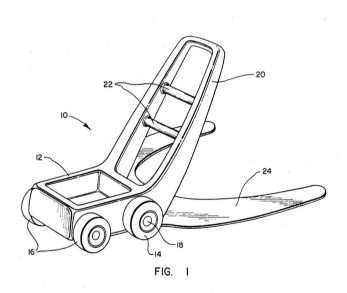

"Child walker-trainer." Patented in 1991 by
Lloyd Baum and Dan Fischer.

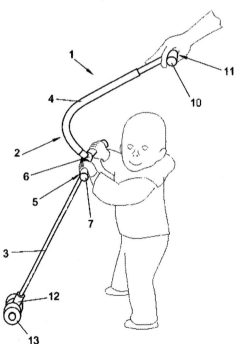

"A baby walking apparatus." Patented in
2011 by Antonio Peron.

Just Hanging Around

There are many useful baby carriers on the market today, but only one that's designed for parents who need to use the bathroom. Whether at the mall, the doctor's office, or even at home, toddlers can get into all sorts of trouble while their parents are taking care of business. Fitted with two metal hooks that conveniently fit over door tops, the BabyKeeper lets a parent suspend their child from a bathroom door, preventing escapes. Patented in 2009 by Tonja King, this invention is a practical device for parents on the go. It hasn't really caught on, though, perhaps because the hanging child will most likely be staring right at their pottying parent? Then there's the slight chance the parent may forget the baby and leave her on the door . . .

Hooked up

This 2010 patent from Louis and Karen Tompros is a "sling comprising a tail portion and two arm portions that support an infant when rings at the ends of the tail and arm are brought together at a single point above the infant. The rings are held together by a clamp, and the clamp allows the sling to be attached to a wall-mounted hook, a ceiling-mounted hook, a door-mounted hook and more."

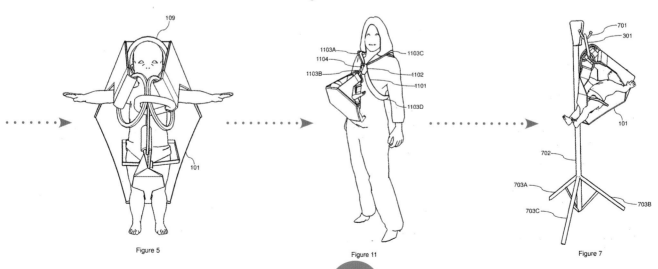

Figure 5   Figure 11   Figure 7

Pockets for Your Pooch

W ho needs a leash when you can wear your favorite pet inside your shirt? As long as you don't own a Rottweiler or a Great Dane, your pet can travel with you anywhere, while both of your arms remain free. Donna Samet patented this invention in 2007.

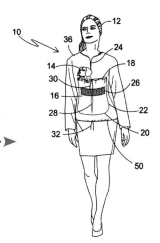

Moo-ve It

W orried about the proper care and transport of newborn cows, Gerald Funk patented this carrier for calves in 1992. Calves can weigh up to 130 pounds at birth, and they often need to be transported to ensure their survival. This carrier not only does the trick, it also provides a "great deal of tender loving care."

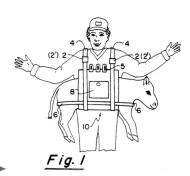

Fig. 1

Puppy Purse

K athy Manuel patented this small animal carrier in 1998. It's basically a dog vest with a strap. When it's time to go, simply pick the dog up by the strap and be on your way. If you place some pockets in the vest, your puppy becomes an instant purse on the run.

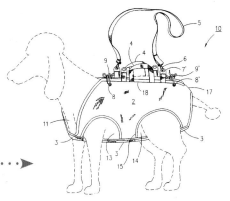

Fig. 6

Short Leash on Life

Although called a "device for use in guiding and supporting children," its more common name is a "leash." There are several patented children's leashes, but this 1940 invention by Edouard Nadeau is notable for its ability to tether one child while giving a slightly older child something to hold onto.

Enjoying Your Ride?

How does one solve the problem of dogs wanting to stick their heads out car windows? Here is one novel, if not extremely dangerous idea. A 1935 issue of *Popular Mechanics* proposed the Dog Sack, which places the dog outside the car completely, fastened to one of the car doors. The dog would rest his legs on running boards (small platforms) along both sides of old cars.

In 1954, another inventor cut a hole in the trunk of his car for his dog to peek through.

The Dog Days ... and Hours

Fig. 1

Since most animals live shorter lives as measured by human time, shouldn't animals have different watches? The inventors of this watch thought so. According to the 1991 patent application by Rodney Metts and Barry Thomas, "a dog that lives ten years has lived a full life; a man might live seventy-seven years . . . This invention is a watch made to run at a time different than human time." So a dog's watch would run seven times faster than a human's watch, since on average a human lives seven times longer than a dog. The usefulness of the watch, according to its inventors, is that pet owners can figure out how long human activities seem to their pets. For instance, "a one-hour ride in an automobile will register seven hours on a dog watch." The watch was never made, probably because it would be confusing for humans, and animals don't care about the time.

We're Out of Time

Okay, technically, we're out of space; however, this dog has been keeping an eye on our progress and has informed us it's time to wrap things up here. We hope this book has inspired you as much as it has us. There are some crazy brilliant, crazy useful, and crazy-crazy inventions in this book, and there are millions more out there that should have changed the world, could have changed the world, would have changed the world . . . but for some reason or another, didn't. Some inventors gave up, while others went on to create something better. The human mind was made for solving problems, and these inventions prove that while not all the inventions we come up with

change the world, they are certainly worth checking out because they may give us an idea that will change it. Good luck and thanks for reading this book!

Will You Change the World?

See a problem out there that needs fixing? Why not invent something? Do your research to see what has already been invented, then come up with your own idea and test it out. If you're happy with the results, patent it. What do you think? Will you change the world?

Resources

Most of the research for this book was done through Google's patents search engine, which is easy to use and quite fun. Check it out at www.google.com/patents.

There are lots of books about inventions and inventors; head to the local library and check them out!

For more information on how patents work, check out http://money.howstuffworks.com/patent.htm.

To read old magazine articles about inventions that could have changed the world but didn't, check out http://blog.modernmechanix.com/.

Interested in wacky inventions? Check out http://www.wackyinventions.com/.

To watch a documentary about failed inventions, check out http://topdocumentaryfilms.com/failed-inventions/.

To get more information on the United States Patent and Trademark Office, check out http://www.uspto.gov/patents/.

To search Canadian patents, check out http://brevets-patents.ic.gc.ca/opic-cipo/cpd/eng/introduction.html.

To search more than 32 million international patents, check out http://patentscope.wipo.int/search/en/search.jsf.

To access all of Thomas Edison's patent applications, check out http://edison.rutgers.edu/patenti1.htm.

For more information on Buckminster Fuller, check out https://bfi.org/about-fuller.

For more information on famous women inventors, check out http://www.women-inventors.com/.

To watch a documentary about inventions that changed the world, check out http://topdocumentaryfilms.com/inventions-changed-world/.

To find out about some kid inventors, check out http://www.cnbc.com/id/42497934#.

PHOTO CREDITS

Subject Index

Inventor Index

"Imagination has brought mankind through the Dark Ages to its present state of civilization. Imagination led Columbus to discover America. Imagination led Franklin to discover electricity. Imagination has given us the steam engine, the telephone, the talking-machine, and the automobile, for these things had to be dreamed of before they became realities. So I believe that dreams—daydreams, you know, with your eyes wide open and your brain-machinery whizzing—are likely to lead to the betterment of the world. The imaginative child will become the imaginative man or woman most apt to create, to invent, and therefore to foster civilization."

~L. Frank Baum, from his book, *The Lost Princess of Oz*